PALACES

MASTERPIECES OF ARCHITECTURE

LAURA BROOKS

TODTRI

This book was designed and produced by TODTRI Book Publishers
P.O. Box 572, New York, NY 10116-0572
FAX: (212) 695-6984
e-mail: info@todtri.com

Printed and bound in Singapore

ISBN 1-57717-146-2

Author: Laura Brooks

Publisher: Robert M. Tod
Senior Editor: Edward Douglas
Associate Editor: Amy Handy
Designer: Mark Weinberg
Typesetting: Command-O, NYC

Visit us on the web!

www.todtri.com

PICTURE CREDITS

Photographer/page number

Picture Perfect
Ace/Clive Friend 13 (top)
Jean Buldain 77 (top)
Charles Bowman 10, 14, 17 (top & bottom), 33, 34 (bottom), 39 (top)
Bill Holden 71 (bottom), 74
Images Colour Library 61 (bottom)
Dave & Les Jacobs 62 , 70
Nawrocki Stock Photo 24–25
Picture Colour Library 34 (top)
Jose Raga 54, 58 (top)
E. Simanor 35
Vadim Sokolov 75, 76
Adina Tovy 40–41

Lee Snider 5, 6, 8–9, 12, 13 (bottom), 16, 20, 21, 22, 23, 26, 27 (top & bottom), 28, 29, 30 (top & bottom), 31 (top & bottom), 32, 36, 37, 39 (bottom), 45, 46 (top), 49 (top & bottom), 50 (top & bottom), 51, 53 (bottom), 55, 61 (top), 66, 67, 68 (top), 69, 72–73

SuperStock 7, 11, 15, 18 (top & bottom), 19, 38, 42 (top & bottom), 43, 44, 46 (bottom), 47, 48, 52, 53 (top), 56–57, 58 (bottom), 59, 60, 63 (top & bottom), 64, 65 (top & bottom), 68 (bottom), 71 (top), 77(bottom), 78, 79

CONTENTS

INTRODUCTION

What is a fitting residence for a head of state or a noble family? This is the question architects, builders, political dignitaries, and members of the aristocracy have asked themselves throughout history. The answer, judging from the spectacular results, is a palace.

The history of the palace is the history of Europe. From Portugal to Russia, palaces serve as a centerpiece for a nation's capital, and grace the countryside with impressive architecture, magical gardens, and illustrious histories. Each palace history is a testament to personal will, political power, immense wealth, luxurious taste, dynastic pride, and family rivalry. These prominent displays of prestige obsessed their original creators, and continue to delight and educate modern visitors around the world.

Historical Highlights

From the beginning of recorded time, political leaders and wealthy individuals have created luxurious residences for themselves, their families, and their closest associates. Some of our knowledge of the early days of ancient Greece comes from archaeological excavations from the Palace of Minos on the island of Crete, a luxurious royal residence constructed about 1500 B.C. Since this ancient Aegean palace already represents palace architecture in full development, one must assume that a tradition of palace-building began long before that, perhaps in ancient Egypt. Palaces are known throughout the ancient world; the palace of Persepolis, built for Darius I around 500 B.C. in Iran, was a complex of courtyards, as well as luxuriously decorated public and private spaces.

Greek and Roman villas continued the tradition of luxurious living among society's elite. The palaces of the Roman emperors included expansive courtyards, fountains, and gardens, a tradition that would continue throughout the history of the palace. Even the more modest Roman residence or *domus* included at least one atrium open to the sky, with a pool for collecting water, and marble statuary to create a stately environment for living. Excavations of imperial residences like the palace of Diocletian in Split and the villas of Pompeii yield valuable information about how the upper class lived during this ancient period.

RIGHT: An exquisite, crown-like spire adorns the pinnacle of Christianborg Palace in Copenhagen, Denmark.

RIGHT: The Palacio Nacional seems to rise out of the hills like a mirage, dominating the urban center of Sintra, Portugal. This palace, begun in the fifteenth century, is known for its unusual double chimney.

But it was in the Middle Ages that the palace as we have come to understand it developed. Concerned first and foremost with security, medieval palace architects constructed a central keep or defensible tower surrounded by outbuildings enclosed within a defensible wall, often surrounded by a moat. The noble family and its entourage lived communally in great halls with open hearths and a few luxurious furnishings such as tapestries, precious metalwork, and simple seating.

By the fourteenth and fifteenth centuries, however, palace architects and inhabitants began to give greater emphasis to private quarters within the palace, and these personal chambers soon equaled the importance of the more public spaces such as meeting and banquet halls. Patrons demanded more deluxe creature comforts, including sumptuously decorated bedchambers, fine furniture, and other amenities. Palaces of the medieval Islamic world, including the legendary caliphal palace in Baghdad and later examples like Spain's Alhambra, take luxurious living to new heights, with opulent tile work, oasislike gardens and courtyards, and magnificent intimate quarters.

The Renaissance and baroque periods—the sixteenth, seventeenth, and eighteenth centuries—represented a golden age in the history of palaces. This heyday of palace building witnessed the construction of masterpieces such as Versailles, Buckingham Palace, the imperial residences of Vienna and St. Petersburg, the Italian merchant palaces, the châteaux of the Loire Valley, and many other luxury residences for royal courts and aristocrats across the Eurasian continent. By the mid-eighteenth century, the prevailing rococo style—characterized by sinuous lines; whimsical decoration featuring shells, cherubs, and scrolls; and more intimate private spaces—became the rage in Europe. Palaces like the Zwinger in Dresden and Queluz in Portugal represent the height of these flights of fancy.

This period of prolific palace building coincided with a gradual shift from small autonomous regions ruled by local leaders to a major consolidation of political power among just a few royal families of Europe. While the feudal system of the Middle Ages relied on petty rulers from leading clans, by the sixteenth and seventeenth centuries the major powers of Europe—England, France, Spain, Prussia, Holland, Russia, Denmark, and Sweden—had been formed. The reigns of power were held in the hands of a very few. It was not unusual to find German Hapsburgs ruling Spain and French Bourbons ruling southern Italy, or for a single family to dispatch representatives to every major royal court of Europe. Alliances between courts were made through marriage, and palaces served as the epicenter of political and family life in this small world.

By the end of the eighteenth century, the age of great palaces came to a close. The Industrial Revolution and the rise of more democratic governments across Europe and America diminished the power of the ruling families, and increasing popular disapproval brought this age of ostentatious display to a gradual end. In France, the Revolution stopped an era of spectacular palace building in its tracks. In 1789, as heads rolled in Paris, the silver furniture that adorned Versailles' famous Hall of Mirrors was melted down.

But palace building did not come to a halt everywhere. Well into the nineteenth century, European nobility continued to construct palaces in certain pockets of Europe. The fantastic creations of Ludwig II of Bavaria—the palaces of Neuschwanstein, Linderhof, and Herrenchiemsee—bear testament to the continued luxury-conscious nature of the aristocracy. Pena Palace, near Sintra, Portugal, provided a nineteenth-century Romantic wonderland for Dom Fernando II. In no case, however, were these patrons breaking new ground in the history of the palace. Instead, each structure reflects a nostalgia for the palaces of a golden age whose time had already come and gone.

City and Country

For royalty, maintaining a presence in the nation's capital was essential for keeping their hands on the reigns of political power. Buckingham Palace in London, the Louvre in Paris, the Imperial Palace in Vienna, and the Royal Palace in Stockholm all served this need. Visiting heads of state and foreign dignitaries were often welcomed into these "capital palaces," entertained with elaborate state dinners and elegant balls.

For many palace inhabitants, however, the pleasures of the countryside beckoned, and many of the most luxurious retreats were constructed far from the capital city. Ludwig II's Linderhof is nestled in a valley of the Bavarian Alps; Peterhof served as the country retreat of the Russian royal family alongside the Baltic Sea; Drottningholm was constructed for the Swedish royal family on a secluded island distant from Stockholm. The Loire Valley of France boasts a high concentration of palaces used as royal hunting retreats for the Parisian nobility. For the British monarchy, spending time in the country has always been fundamental. While Buckingham Palace serves as the official residence of the monarchs in London, the royal family has retreated for centuries to Windsor and other rural estates whenever possible.

The opposite was true in eighteenth-century France. By 1700 the nobility tired of life at the court of Versailles shadowing an aging Louis XIV. Many royal attendants moved from this vast country estate back into Paris, where they built smaller but equally sumptuous residences, or *hôtels,* in a rococo style emphasizing serpentine lines and cohesive decorative schemes in which painting, sculpture, porcelain, and furniture all played a part. For them, the excitement of city life outweighed the pleasures of the country, which had grown dull over the near century-long rule of this commanding monarch.

Some palaces were used only during certain seasons of the year. The châteaux of the Loire Valley, for example, were inhabited primarily in the fall, when noble families and their guests took advantage of hunting in the vast woods surrounding each palace. The château of Chambord displays a stunning chandelier of deer antlers in one hall, a reference to the primary function of these luxurious country homes. Other palaces, such as the Portuguese palace of Queluz and the Schönnbrun Palace in Vienna, served primarily as summer retreats. Caretakers lived on the property year round to keep up the buildings and their maintenance-intensive, parklike grounds.

RIGHT: A bird's-eye view of the Palace of Versailles gives a sense of the vastness of the palace and its grounds. The artist, Pierre Patel, created this rendering during the seventeenth century, at the height of the court life at the palace.

FOLLOWING PAGE: The Grand Staircase at the Residenz Palace in Wurzburg is renowned for its fabulous ceiling painted by the Venetian artist, Tiepolo.

In other cases, certain parts of a palace were used only in certain seasons. The ground floor of the Pitti Palace in Florence, for example, served as the grand ducal apartment only in the summertime; during the rest of the year the grand duke made his chambers on the upper floors. Vast palaces were difficult and costly to heat, and many inhabitants chose to confine their activities to a certain number of rooms during the cold months.

Spaces Sublime and Mundane

Palaces are rarely the result of a single vision, and are almost always in a state of construction, reconstruction, or restoration. Each inhabitant adds his or her own personal touch to the family estate. The oldest, most venerable palaces—Fontainebleau, Hampton Court, Windsor, and others—are agglomerations of centuries of architectural styles and construction. Each palace is a living lesson in the history of taste, style, architectural design, and cults of personality.

Palaces vary dramatically from place to place, but it is possible to outline some of their most common features. They are often based on a square or rectangular plan, frequently incorporating one or more courtyards. This emphasis on the courtyard—large, open spaces for meetings, ceremonies, parties, military formations, and other purposes—has been fundamental to palace architecture from the beginning of recorded history. From the ancient Palace of Minos on the island of Crete to the Roman villa and the medieval Islamic palace, the courtyard has been a central feature of the palace. In many cases courtyards are synonymous with water, since they incorporate an oasis of fountains, pools, plants, and trees. Many palaces

contain more than one of these spaces; the palace of Hampton Court counts thirteen courtyards within its extensive complex.

Palaces usually include a variety of "public" spaces for receiving guests, hosting events, and conducting official business. Great halls, such as the Hall of Mirrors at Versailles, trace their origins to the Middle Ages, when such a space served as the heart of the palace. Ballrooms appeared by the Renaissance and baroque periods to accommodate the many dances, masquerades, and other balls popular during that era.

In the banquet halls of palaces across Europe, official dinners were and still are occasions of the utmost pomp and ceremony. One glance at the extensive silver, crystal, and china collections of many palaces confirms the importance of these meals, which gather not only the royal family but often foreign dignitaries and other important heads of state. The Imperial Palace in Vienna displays the so-called Milan Centerpiece, a table decoration nearly 98 feet long, as well as complete table settings for 140 guests.

Palaces also encompass a variety of more private spaces, sometimes including personal "apartments" within the larger complex of the palace. It was customary for husbands and wives to maintain separate quarters, and in fact, a queen and her attendants might occupy a wing of the palace completely apart from her husband and his entourage. In a vast palace such as Versailles, this might represent a considerable distance. A typical apartment might contain a bedroom, dressing room, and a special drawing room for writing correspondence or receiving guests. Each apartment might also be adjoined by rooms for attendants or valets. These intimate spaces were usually sumptuously decorated with billowing fabrics, luxurious tapestries, and fine furniture.

A palace chapel was customary, especially in larger palaces. Like the great hall, the chapel was a holdover from the Middle Ages. These were often used for private religious services, and a member of the clergy might be engaged as a member of the household especially for this purpose. The chapel might also serve as the locus for marriages, baptisms, and funerals. The palace chapels at Versailles and the Escorial are among the largest palace chapels. The Escorial also maintains a separate pantheon for royal burials in a designated area of the palace.

In addition, many other specialized rooms appear throughout palaces. Music rooms and palace theaters were sometimes included in palace plans because entertainment served an important function for the palace community. Music was an important part of noblewomen's education, and many palace women were accomplished on the violin or spinet. Frederick the Great joined palace musicians on the flute at his residence at Sans Souci in Potsdam, playing the works of Bach and

ABOVE: Originally conceived in the seventeenth century as a grandiose town hall, the Royal Palace of Amsterdam has been used for official royal functions since 1808.

Mozart. Louis XIV participated in theatrical ballet performances at Versailles. Mozart performed for the court throughout his life in the imperial palaces of Vienna. The Swedish palace of Drottningholm drew renowned French and Italian acting troupes to its large theater. King Ludwig II was devoted to the works of Richard Wagner, incorporating many of the composer's themes into the rooms of the palace itself.

Libraries are also a common feature of larger palaces. In many cases, the library began with the personal collection of the palace builder, and later became important repository for state documents, valuable historical manuscripts, and other important printed books and maps. The Escorial outside Madrid began with the extensive collection of Philip II. The Imperial Palace in Vienna and the Royal Palace in Naples also house important collections.

Palace furnishings almost always went beyond what was necessary to live. In addition to places to sit, eat, sleep, play music, converse, play cards, or other activities, palace furnishings usually included a variety of tapestries, porcelains, gilded sculpture, clocks, candelabras, chandeliers, and other fixtures. In royal palaces, such as Versailles and the Royal Palace in Madrid, it was customary to support royal tapestry and porcelain factories either on palace property or nearby. These production houses created precious objects expressly for the needs of the court. The famous Gobelins tapestry works in Paris and the Sèvres porcelain factory gained worldwide prominence in this manner.

In addition to the public and private spaces in which the nobility circulated, quarters and work areas for servants were often extensive. Kitchens, bake houses, wash houses, and other utilitarian spaces were often large and sometimes even constituted separate buildings. The open hearths in the kitchens at Hampton Court were large enough to roast a whole ox, and it is easy to imagine the crowds of servants it must have required to service a palace of that size. Servants' living quarters were usually modest and most importantly unobtrusive, so that the staff could circulate without crossing paths with the noble families for whom they worked.

Every important palace had a garden. Beyond the palace walls, these oases of exotic trees, flowers, shrubs, and fountains were the pride of palace owners. In the late Middle Ages the palace gardens were often an extension of the vast hunting preserves that surrounded the palace, but by the seventeenth and eighteenth centuries the concept of the garden had been transformed. The meticulously maintained gardens such as those found at Versailles and Chenonceaux represent the Enlightenment's ideal of man's control of nature. The various geometric patterns created by clipping boxwood hedges, color-coordinated flower beds, and sculpted topiary trees all required a full-time professional gardening staff. Many nobles spent hours a day strolling through the gardens and lighting at specially constructed pavilions or "cottages" scattered around the vast, parklike grounds.

In addition to the customary features of the palace, palace owners sometimes ordered special, unusual spaces. The Tudor king Henry VIII built a bowling alley and tennis courts at Hampton Court. The Schönbrunn Palace in Vienna includes a zoo. Whatever their configuration, each palace is a unique creation, representing the tastes and vision of many individuals across the generations of aristocratic families.

CHAPTER ONE

ROYAL RESIDENCES: GREAT BRITAIN AND SCANDINAVIA

People have always been fascinated by the lifestyles of royalty, especially Britain's royal family. Modern media has made the monarch's extended family the focus of overwhelming public interest and intense scrutiny never dreamed possible in past centuries. Still, life inside the walls of Britain's royal palaces has a private component as well as a public facade.

The British have long had a tradition of elegant country living, and in England, the concept of the country house was fully developed by the sixteenth century. More elaborate royal residences of the seventeenth and eighteenth centuries, whether in the city or the country, tend to focus on symmetry, as can be seen from the exteriors of Buckingham Palace and Hampton Court. Like many other palaces across Europe, each dwelling represents the collective vision of the people who inhabited these opulent spaces.

Majestic Abodes

One of the world's best-known royal residences is Buckingham Palace. The palace owes its fame partly to the fact that it still stands as a residence of a head of state, and partly because of its location—in the center of London. Today, one of the highlights of a tour of London is the changing of the guard at Buckingham Palace.

From the time that James I planted a large tract of land in the Pimlico section of London with mulberry trees, hoping to start a silk boom in Britain, the area has been inhabited by royals. The Duke of Buckingham, for whom the palace is named, played only a minor role in the history of this vast estate. His third wife, the illegitimate daughter of James II, lived in a grand house on the edge of the mulberry grove for twenty-one years after the duke's death. George III bought the house from her,

ABOVE: According to some witnesses, the tranquility of Hampton Court's corridors is sometimes interrupted by the fleeting apparition of Catherine Howard, wife of Henry VIII, who was executed here in 1542.

LEFT: In 1535, King James II ordered the construction of this majestic gateway to Linlithgow Palace in Scotland.

LEFT: A royal crest adorns the main gate at Buckingham Palace in London. The lion and the unicorn have long been symbols of the British monarchy.

and henceforth it became the main residence of the British royal family.

Behind its stark, neoclassical facades and vast, empty central courtyard lies a complex network of sumptuously decorated drawing rooms, banquet halls, ballrooms, and private chambers. The queen holds the most valuable and expansive private art collection in the world, and many of the works by Leonardo, Raphael, Titian, and other masters are housed at Buckingham Palace.

In spite of its location in the heart of this massive, sprawling city, Buckingham Palace was meant to make its residents feel that they were out in the country. In stark contrast to its main facade overlooking the city, the back of the building opens out to expansive, parklike grounds that transport the visitor miles away from the hustle and bustle of modern London.

Fourteen miles outside London, Hampton Court stands among the most stunning of British royal residences. Begun as a manor house given to Henry VIII in 1525 by Cardinal Thomas Wolsey, Hampton Court would become an extensive complex along the Thames River. Already enlarged by Henry VIII in the sixteenth century, William and Mary made Hampton Court their primary residence. They engaged the services of the architect Sir Christopher Wren to create a grandiose building with expansive gardens that would rival those of the French court at Versailles. Wren spent forty-eight years working toward that goal.

Hampton Court served as a regal country retreat and hunting lodge for many royals. The striking red brick and stone exterior

visitors see today replaced Henry VIII's former palace, though vestiges of the Tudor structure remain. The eight-acre complex houses thirteen inner courtyards, offering dramatic vistas of the various wings and outbuildings of this impressive palace.

Interior luxuries include a magnificent collection of tapestries, which were rehung regularly to provide an ever-changing display along the hallways and chambers of this vast complex. His-and-hers staircases lead to the king and queen's personal chambers. Servants worked in a massive kitchen with an eighteen-foot-long open hearth to feed the royals and their entourage. The expansive grounds include formal flower beds, ponds, and fountains reflecting more than three hundred years of English garden design.

Hampton Court echoes with the memory of Henry VIII's first two wives. The initials of Anne Boleyn once graced the Tudor courtyards of the palace, but were erased from its walls after she was executed on charges of adultery. Another of the king's wives—Catherine Howard—was also accused of adultery and executed at Hampton Court in 1542. Legend has it that the screaming ghost of Catherine can be seen running through the galleries of the sprawling palace.

Unlikely Beginnings

What began in the Middle Ages as a hospital for women with leprosy in the marshy lands beyond Westminster in London became one of the most cherished of Britain's royal residences—St. James's Palace. By 1532, after the deadly disease had declined and the hospital counted only four inmates, King

LEFT: Hampton Court sprawls along the Thames River outside of London. The enormous palace boasts no less than 13 interior courtyards and its kitchen has an open hearth large enough to roast an ox.

RIGHT: An imposing neoclassical facade at London's Buckingham Palace belies an interior of sumptuously decorated halls, chambers, and private quarters for the royal family. What began as a grove of silk trees planted by James I emerged as the primary residence of the British monarchs.

Henry VIII acquired and endowed the hospital as a traditional royal act of charity. The king rebuilt the hospital, and added a royal residence that became a favorite retreat for Anne Boleyn.

The palace retains its Tudor core around the courtyards, as well as a walled park that the king used for hunting deer. Smaller and more private than many of the larger royal residences, many monarchs in later generations made St. James's a secluded retreat. The architect Inigo Jones and others enlarged the palace, and the Tudor park was made larger and more grand by André Le Nôtre, who also designed gardens at Versailles.

Many royal births and weddings took place at St. James's, including the joining in marriage of Queen Victoria and Prince Albert, in the palace's small chapel. The palace remains a royal residence for more junior members of court, who live inside the walls of a building with a long and illustrious history.

Country Retreats

For centuries in Britain, royalty have regarded their residences in the capital cities of London and Edinburgh as

ABOVE: Manicured grounds surround Kensington Palace, including an intimate sunken garden that served as an oasis for the palace's inhabitants. Like Windsor Castle, Kensington served as a pastoral retreat for royals wishing to escape the bustle of city life.

mere pieds-à-terre, considering their great royal country estates their real homes. British hearts lie in the rolling green countryside, and rural palaces like Windsor have been lavishly adorned and cherished by the royal family for centuries.

Kensington Palace is just one of many royal residences that satisfied the desire of the royal family to retreat from the hustle and bustle of life at court in London. William and Mary chose Kensington as their country estate in 1689, enlisting the services of architect Sir Christopher Wren to enlarge an already existing residence built by the Earl of Nottingham. Mary saw to it that gardeners planted twenty-six acres of flower beds in a formal French style, with expansive parks and views into the countryside.

The house was enlarged under George I, and the gardens and ponds were further expanded, providing much of what is today Hyde Park and Kensington Gardens. Queen Victoria was born at Kensington and spent much of her childhood there, sleeping in the same chambers with her mother until she was named monarch.

Upon leaving her childhood home to assume the throne at Buckingham Palace, the newly crowned Queen Victoria wrote:

> Though I rejoice to go into B.P. [Buckingham Palace] for many reasons, it is not without feeling of regret that I shall bid adieu for ever (that is to say for ever as a dwelling), to this my birth-place, where I have been born and bred, and to which I am really attached. . . . I have gone through painful and disagreeable scenes here, 'tis true, but still I am fond of the poor old Palace.

Later the Queen opened the building to the public, and it can still be toured today.

BELOW: Queen Anne had Blenheim Palace built for John Churchill, first Duke of Marlborough, as a reward for his triumph at the Battle of Blenheim. The victory saved Vienna from an invasion by Louis XIV's French army in 1704.

LEFT: The interior of Blenheim Palace reflects eighteenth-century taste for the neoclassical style. Its architect, John Vanbrugh, said that the building should possess the qualities of "beauty, magnificence and duration."

RIGHT: An impressionistic rendering of Windsor Castle gives a sense of the enormity of this sprawling estate. Windsor is the only English royal residence in continuous use since the Middle Ages, and is a favorite retreat for today's monarch.

ABOVE: The King's State Bed Chamber at Windsor Castle is bedecked with everything one would expect of a monarch's private quarters—great art, decorative moldings, an elegant mantle, and sumptuous furniture. Here, the imposing bed canopy is topped by a crown.

One of the most famous of Britain's royal country palaces is Windsor Castle. It is also among the oldest, first constructed in 1080 by William the Conqueror. Rebuilt over subsequent centuries, nearly every British monarch has made his or her mark at Windsor. Today it is the only English royal residence in continuous use since the Middle Ages.

Highlights include a circular banqueting hall with a round table built by Edward III in 1344, based on his fascination with King Arthur's Knights of the Round Table. Saint George's Chapel displays a stunning fan-vaulted ceiling begun by Edward IV in the 1470s.

It is thought that the cesspools surrounding the palace as well as the medieval drainage system contributed to the typhoid fever that killed Prince Albert at Windsor in 1861. His room was left intact for forty years, including freshly pressed clothes and a glass from which he had taken his last medication.

Today, visitors can view many parts of Windsor, though it remains very much a living palace for the current royal family, who spend weekends and extended holidays at Windsor among the memories and relics of their forefathers, as well as a splendid art collection that includes an extensive accumulation of drawings by Leonardo da Vinci.

ABOVE: St. George's Hall at Windsor Castle serves as a primary reception area for official guests. The thrones of the reigning monarch and his or her spouse, sit majestically before an impressive screen decorated with royal crests.

ABOVE: Massive stone towers greet visitors to Falkland Palace in Falkland, Scotland. The palace was the country estate and hunting lodge of eight Stuart monarchs, including Mary, Queen of Scots.

RIGHT: A sculpted unicorn–part of the royal crest–greets visitors at the gate of Holyrood Palace in Edinburgh, Scotland. It has been a royal palace since James IV chose the city as his capital.

A Checkered Past

Holyrood Palace in Edinburgh, Scotland, took its name from a medieval abbey on the property that held a relic of the True Cross or "Rood." The Scottish monarchs had long lodged in the small castle adjacent to the abbey by the time that James IV chose Edinburgh as Scotland's capital and made Holyrood a royal palace. Today the palace retains that status. Scotland's close ties with France during this early period manifest themselves in the architecture of Holyrood—its turrets and round towers bring to mind the châteaux of the Loire valley.

Mary, Queen of Scots, chose Holyrood as her principal residence after the death of her husband, the French king Francis II. The palace formed a backdrop for a dramatic conspiracy in the 1560s that led to the murder of the popular queen's secretary, David Rizzio, at the hands of Mary's second husband, Lord Darnley, in the queen's private dining room. Lord Darnley himself met a violent end when his own house was later "mysteriously" blown up. Touring the site of Rizzio's murder in the 1840s, Queen Victoria commented that Holyrood was "a princely and most beautiful place."

BELOW: The architecture of Holyrood, with its round towers and turrets, bring to mind the châteaux of the Loire valley, bearing witness to close ties between the Scottish and French royal families.

LEFT: A reproduction of the fantastically ornate fountain from Linlithgow Palace stands at Holyrood.

FOLLOWING PAGE: Blenheim Palace is one of England's largest houses, and includes expansive gardens with countless botanical specimens.

ABOVE: The ceremony of the changing of the guard at Sweden's Royal Palace is a highlight for many visitors to Stockholm.

Northern Lights

After the 1648 Treaty of Westphalia launched the Swedish monarchy among the major European powers, Queen Hedwig Eleonora of Sweden had Drottningholm Palace constructed in 1662 on the island of Lovö. In the mysterious white light of Scandinavia, the effect of this majestic residence emerging from the mist is unforgettable.

French architects Tessin, father and son, designed the palace, complete with grandiose symmetry, mirrored halls, formal gardens, and reflecting ponds. Large portions of the gardens remain intact, and today the Renaissance bronze sculptures and manicured, parklike grounds still reflect their original grandeur. Treasures of the palace's interior include a grand staircase and the luxurious state bedchamber where Hedwig Eleonora slept.

After Queen Hedwig Eleonora's reign, monarchs over the next two hundred years left their mark on Drottningholm. During the mid-eighteenth century, Drottningholm enjoyed a facelift under the artistic patronage of Queen Louisa Ulrika, wife of Swedish King Adolf Fredrik. At a time when all things Asian influenced European designers, Louisa Ulrika received a gift from her husband of a delightful "Chinese Pavilion," a small, elegant structure resembling a dollhouse and filled with the latest chinoiserie by renowned artists. A riot of fanciful, French-inspired rococo decoration characterizes the renovations of Louisa Ulrika, including the queen's antechamber, a library with a renowned collection, and a theater inside the palace. The queen hired French and Italian acting troupes to perform before the court.

After the assassination of King Gustav III in 1792 at a masked ball, the Swedish monarchs ceased visits to Drottningholm, but since 1981 the current royal family has spent summers in the centuries-old palace. Recently the theater has been revived and eighteenth-century plays are performed just as they were in Louisa Ulrika's day.

About a fifty-minute boat ride from the magical island retreat of Drottningholm is the centrally located Royal Palace in Stockholm, which remains the official residence of the Swedish royal family. The history of the palace is ancient.

LEFT: Drottning-holm Palace, located on the enchanting island of Lovö, 50 miles from Stockholm, serves as the primary residence for today's Swedish royal family. The palace was begun in 1662 under Queen Hedwig Eleonora.

LEFT: The elegant gardens surrounding Drottningholm Palace remain faithful to the original designs of the architects Tessin, a French father-and-son team. The patterned plantings, reflecting ponds, and bronze sculptures retain their sense of grandeur and unwavering symmetry.

Vestiges of a fortress on the site thought to date at least to the tenth century prove that the site was important early in Sweden's history. By the fourteenth century, King Magnus Eriksson had constructed a palace there, some of which survives today in the north wing of the present building.

During the Renaissance, under the reign of the Vasa royal family, the palace was largely rebuilt, and more work was begun at the end of the seventeenth century by the architect Nicodemus Tessin the Younger, who had already worked at Drottningholm. Damage from a devastating fire during the construction meant that the royal family vacated the palace for nearly sixty years, and Tessin's plans were not completed until the 1730s. The Great Gallery is in the style of the Hall of Mirrors at Versailles, and was in fact executed by a team of French architects and craftspeople.

In addition to the royal residence, the palace houses the Swedish parliament as well as the national library. Today the palace remains the seat of the royal court and serves as a backdrop for state receptions and events.

Sweden's neighbor, Denmark, also boasts impressive palaces. The palace of Rosenborg in Copenhagen was constructed by Christian IV between 1606 and 1634 in the capital city. Already by the eighteenth century, Rosenborg became less of a royal residence and more of a storehouse for the country's royal treasures, including its crown jewels. Since it was transferred to state ownership in 1849, Rosenborg has been open for public tours of the palace's impressive collections.

ABOVE: The Great Gallery of the Royal Palace in Stockholm was modeled on the Hall of Mirrors at Versailles. The Swedish monarchs brought a team of French architects and craftspeople to execute this expansive wing of the palace.

RIGHT: Rosenborg Palace in Copenhagen, Denmark became the capital residence of Christian IV, who had the palace constructed between 1606 and 1634.

ABOVE: A statue of Frederick II on horse-back stands before Amalienborg Palace in Copenhagen, Denmark. The equestrian portrait has been popular with rulers since ancient Rome.

RIGHT: Colorful royal Danish thrones adorn Christianborg Palace in Copenhagen.

ABOVE: Formal gardens at Rosenborg Palace in Copenhagen provide a dramatic backdrop for the intricate turrets, spires, and decorative brickwork of the palace itself.

LEFT: This extravagant chamber adorns Rosenborg Palace in Copenhagen. Today the public can view the palace's impressive collections, including the Danish crown jewels.

CHAPTER TWO

PAGEANTRY AND SPLENDOR: FRANCE, ITALY, PORTUGAL, AND SPAIN

Southern Europe boasts some of the most impressive palaces in the world. Already in the late Middle Ages and early Renaissance, wealthy merchants and nobles erected luxurious residences in the city-states that now make up Italy—the Medici family in Florence, and the reigning doge in Venice, for example. On the Iberian peninsula, aristocrats and royals of the sixteenth and seventeenth centuries must have been familiar with the Roman villas and opulent Moorish palaces that preceded their own luxury palaces.

In France, Versailles set the standard for palace building, and for centuries to come Louis XIV's vision would be emulated from France to Russia. Finally, the Loire Valley contains one of the highest concentrations of luxury palaces in all of Europe.

The Loire Valley

The Loire Valley of France—a verdant, undulating landscape of vineyards, forests, and meadows—is synonymous with French royalty and palatial residences. During the fifteenth and sixteenth centuries, royalty and nobility were drawn to the fertile hunting grounds afforded by acres of forests inhabited by deer, rabbit, wolves, and other game. They were lured away from city life into the peaceful countryside, where they created their own kingdoms in this region so densely packed with palaces.

One of the trailblazers of this era was King Francis I. A generous patron of the arts, the king was fascinated with Italian culture and brought many of the most innovative artists of the Italian Renaissance—Rosso Fiorentino and Primaticcio, for example—to the French court. Under his patronage, the court of France enjoyed a flourishing of the arts that has been matched by few other monarchs. Among his palatial commissions are the well-known palaces of Chambord and Blois, as well as the reconstruction of the palace of Fontainebleau.

Chambord was constructed for Francis I beginning in 1519, and more than eighteen hundred workers toiled for fifteen years before the palace was complete. Chambord served pri-

LEFT: At Chambord in the Loire Valley, ornate spires adorn the complex system of circular towers and turrets.

ABOVE: Chateau Chambord in the Loire Valley of France appears like a giant wedding cake hidden deep within the forests of western France. The castle served as a hunting lodge for the royal family and their guests.

RIGHT: Formal gardens spread outward from the charming palace of Chenonceaux in the Loire Valley. Boxwoods, topiaries, stone paths, and colorful annuals create dynamic patterns to delight the eye.

marily as a hunting lodge. At its core is a square keep marked on four corners with round towers, a design that recalls medieval castle architecture. But these Renaissance architects, some of whom were brought from Italy, created a more complex plan. A profusion of turrets, chimneys, and dormers—all lavishly decorated with sculpture—emerge from the roof of Chambord, giving the palace the appearance of a giant wedding cake.

One of the highlights of Chambord's interior is the double-spiral staircase, in which two staircases intertwine around the same axis but never actually meet. This tour-de-force has been attributed to a design by Leonardo da Vinci. The vast kitchens on the lowest level were equipped to cook the bounty of the hunt and serve it to guests in the vast banquet hall.

Francis I also was responsible for a large part of the palace of Blois, also in the Loire Valley. Blois is known for its famous external octagonal staircase, a masterpiece of architecture designed by François Mansart between 1635 and 1638. The stairway opens to a large courtyard designed during the reign of Francis I, where the visitor can appreciate three levels of intricate sculptural detail and a play of mass and composition. The staircase appears like an open cage of sculpture and architecture.

Much of the magic of the palace of Chenonceaux is due to its situation across the Cher river itself. A four-towered keep on the edge of the river, designed at the beginning of the sixteenth century, was enlarged by extending the building out over the river itself along a massive bridge designed by Philibert de l'Orme at mid-century. Diane de Poitiers was responsible for

ABOVE: The chateau of Chenonceaux stands astride the river Cher in the Loire Valley. Diane de Poitiers ordered its construction, and served as mistress of this fairy-tale palace.

RIGHT: The famous external octagonal stairway at Blois opens onto a large courtyard. Its unusual structure and sculptural detail form a masterful play of mass and composition.

the construction of the palace on the bridge. Images of Diane personified as Diana the Huntress—a fitting allegory for the hunting life associated with the Loire Valley—can be found throughout the palace. Formal gardens extend out from the river, and every spring brings a fragrant display of colorful tulips, clipped boxwood hedges, and delightful topiary designs.

Parisian Palaces

Since the earliest French monarchs of the Middle Ages, Paris has formed the center of court life. The only exception to this rule came in the seventeenth century, when courtiers followed Louis XIV to his country estate in Versailles. Within a century, however, the court moved back into the French capital.

Though most modern visitors to Paris associate the Louvre with some of the world's greatest artistic masterpieces, the building itself began as France's royal palace in the Middle Ages. Originating as a fortress in the twelfth century, the Louvre was built with massive walls surrounded by a moat along the river Seine. While the foundations of this building can still be seen today in the basement of the Louvre, visitors above ground can appreciate centuries of building from the street.

LEFT: The Richlieu Pavilion at the Louvre in Paris provides just one of many impressive facades of this remarkable palace. Most French monarchs from the twelfth century onward left a legacy at this royal-residence-turned-museum.

ABOVE: Dramatically lit at night, the Cour Carrée or "square court" of the Louvre greets the swarm of visitors who come year-round to see one of the world's greatest palaces and museums.

Enlarged by Francis I, the Louvre was further extended by future monarchs. While Louis XIV lost interest in the palace in favor of his beloved Versailles, during the reign of his successor, Louis XV, the work was reinitiated. The western wing of the palace, the Tuileries, was demolished in 1871, but visitors can still appreciate its manicured gardens and fountains. Since 1793 the Louvre has served as one of the world's greatest art museums.

Just beyond Paris, Fontainebleau stands among the most venerable palaces in France. The forest of Fontainebleau—which still lures visitors to its nearly fifty thousand acres—provided fertile hunting grounds for monarchs as early as the twelfth century. Philip the Fair was born there in 1268, and the king died after falling from a horse during a hunt in the forests of the royal palace. Francis I lavished his attention on Fontainebleau after 1527, inviting Italian architects, sculptors, and painters to the site. Primaticcio, Rosso Fiorentino, Vignola, Serlio, and other well-known artists made their mark on the palace. Over the course of the seventeenth and eighteenth centuries, monarchs continued to embellish Fontainebleau with new wings, lavish gardens, furniture, and other objects. Napoleon restored the palace at the beginning of the nineteenth century, and signed his abdication there in 1814.

LEFT: Before its destruction in the nineteenth century, the artist Jean Louis Ernest Meissonier captured the ruins of the Tuileries Palace, which formed the western wing of the Louvre in Paris.

ABOVE: Fontainebleau is one of the most venerable palaces of France, and nearly every monarch since the twelfth century has made a mark on the palace and the fertile hunting grounds that surround it.

LEFT: The gardens of the former Tuileries Palace serve today as a tranquil gathering place for Parisians and visitors within an otherwise modern, bustling city.

FOLLOWING PAGE: The château of Blois is one of the gems of France's Loire Valley. King Francis I, a tireless patron of the arts, was responsible in part for its construction.

RIGHT: A view through the main gate at Versailles offers visitors a mere glimpse of the immense architectural and garden complex that lies beyond it.

RIGHT: The palace of Versailles is surrounded by acres of neatly manicured grounds, fountains with bronze sculptures, and outbuildings that constitute small palaces in themselves.

Versailles

Versailles is pure theater. What began as a humble hunting lodge outside Paris for Louis XIII became for his son—the illustrious Louis XIV—not only a political statement but a spectacular inspiration for palace architects all over Europe. Under Louis XIV, who ruled there until 1715, Versailles represented the cutting edge of seventeenth-century palace design. The man who claimed "I am the State" and referred to himself as the Sun King orchestrated a spectacular architectural and cultural achievement that would be emulated throughout Europe over the next two hundred years.

Today's visitor glimpses only a fraction of the palace from the imposing golden gates at the palace entrance. Once inside, it becomes clear that Versailles actually encompasses a spectrum of buildings on a vast estate. The chapel rivals many of Europe's greatest churches, both in its scale and in the

ABOVE: The Hall of Mirrors at Versailles is one of the most memorable spaces in the palace. A row of mirrors on one side of the hall reflects the vast gardens that sprawl beyond the windows on the opposite side.

sumptuousness of its decoration. The flood of light through the chapel windows illuminates the superb integration of painting, sculpture, and architecture in the space.

Though many architects and craftspeople worked on Versailles, Jules Hardouin Mansart oversaw the main story of the central building between 1678 and 1684. The most well known of Mansart's creations is the Hall of Mirrors, stretching for more than two hundred feet and overlooking the expansive grounds from grand windows from one side, reflecting in the long series of mirrors on the other. The radiant effects of light in the hall were sought after by monarchs and palace builders thereafter.

Political power lay at the center of the king's message, which he expressed through the architecture of Versailles and his own embellished behavior. The king's bedroom stood at the epicenter of the palace, overlooking the gardens. It is here that each morning and evening an elaborate ritual of courtiers surrounded the "rising" and "setting" of the Sun King. The king associated himself with the god Apollo, a figure represented throughout the palace in painting and sculpture, driving his chariot across the sky heralding the dawn.

The gardens of Versailles have proved equally if not more influential on the history of palace design than the building itself. André Le Nôtre—the son of the royal gardener at the Tuileries— designed the garden plan with stunning clarity of vision. Beginning in 1667, Le Nôtre created an axial design radiating from the center of the palace that also mirrored the rising and setting of the sun, cutting through woods, ponds, and formal gardens for acres around the palace. Waterways, ponds, and fountains are filled and lined with statuary of mythological themes. The garden design represents the ultimate taming of nature.

BELOW: In a courtyard at Versailles, outside of Paris, France, marble paving stones and pink facades add a whimsical touch to this otherwise imposing group of buildings and gardens.

RIGHT: In this ornate bedchamber, Louis XIV staged elaborate ceremonies that coincided with his own waking and sleeping. Known as the "Sun King," Louis XIV likened himself to the mythic god Apollo, who heralded each dawn by driving his chariot across the sky.

ABOVE: Queen Marie Antoinette created this fairy-tale mill on the grounds of Versailles, where she and her attendants "played peasant" in a pastoral setting adjacent to the palace's more formal gardens.

RIGHT: Versailles' fountains put on a spectacular display of water and light when they are activated. Each fountain includes marble and bronze sculptures created by sculptors engaged by King Louis XIV in the seventeenth century.

Throughout the vast gardens other small palaces appear. The Petit Trianon—a small private house set amidst the gardens—was a favorite retreat of Marie Antoinette. The abode reflects the interest in smaller, more intimate and decorative spaces that defined eighteenth-century taste.

Palaces of Italy

The story of the Pitti Palace of Florence begins with family rivalry. Undertaken in the late fifteenth century under Luca Pitti, the imposing Pitti Palace has long stood at the heart of Florentine history. Legend holds that the ostentatious palace

ABOVE: The Pitti Palace stands amid the expansive Boboli Gardens on the edge of Florence, Italy. The palace served as the official residence of the city's grand ducal family.

was a blatant form of one-upmanship on the part of the Pitti family, jealous of their former friends and rivals, the Medicis. Once the fortunes of the Pitti faded, however, Cosimo I de Medici and his wife, Eleonora of Toledo, purchased the palace with Eleonora's dowry in 1549, and it became the official residence of the grand ducal family in Florence.

The architect Bartolommeo Ammanati enlarged the palace between 1558 and 1570. With its rustic masonry, the courtyard gives the impression of a heavy, muscular architecture of three stories, with engaged columns and heavy stones quarried from the Boboli Hill on which the building stands. The grand duke made his chambers on one side of the building, while the wife of the grand duke had her own chambers in the lateral wings of the palace. Children's rooms were in a separate area of the building.

Behind the palace stand the Boboli Gardens, a sloping expanse of formal gardens, wooded areas, meandering paths, delightful outbuildings, and trickling fountains. The modern visitor to Florence can stroll through these gardens, as well as visit the eight separate museums that now make up the Pitti Palace and house some of the world's greatest paintings by Italian Renaissance masters such as Raphael and Titian.

Another Italian palace with impressive collections is the Royal Palace of Naples. It was begun about 1600 and remained under construction for the first half of the century. The palace served as the seat of the monarchy in southern Italy, housing the Spanish and Austrian viceroys, the Bourbon kings, and the royal house of Savoy, who ruled over southern Italy at various times. The palace, with its distinctive pink and gray facade of classical decorative elements, overlooks the sea.

During the seventeenth century, the Royal Palace of Naples was more than the seat of government and a residence for the royal family and staff. It functioned as a veritable city of industry. Inside its compound were the royal print works, the royal tapestry factory, the court upholsterers, and the military guard. Since the 1920s, the building has housed the Vittorio Emanuele III National Library, with an extraordinary collection of 1.5 million volumes.

Finally, one of the most visually stunning palaces on the Italian peninsula is the so-called Palazzo Ducale or Doge's Palace of Venice, built alongside the famous basilica of San Marco. The palace presents a fabulous example of late Gothic construction with a Venetian twist: an eastern flavor that pervades many of the medieval and Renaissance buildings of Venice. The exterior is formed by lilting arcades and light pink stone, making the structure appear deceivingly delicate. Venice was ruled by an elected doge, who served for life, along with a Great Council of aristocrats. The palace consists of a variety of state rooms and council halls, as well as a torture chamber and prison.

RIGHT: Venice's Ducal Palace, also called the Palace of the Doge, forms a backdrop for a ceremonious reception of the French ambassador in this painting by the Venetian artist Giovanni Antonio Canaletto, painted in the eighteenth century.

ABOVE: The Ocean Fountain, designed in 1576 by Giovanni da Bologna, stands in the Boboli Gardens at the Pitti Palace in Florence, Italy.

LEFT: Grandiose statues of Mars and Neptune guard the entryway to the Ducal Palace in Venice. The winged lion is a symbol of Saint Mark, patron saint of this important port city.

RIGHT: The opulent Royal Palace of Queluz in Portugal reflects eighteenth-century taste for whimsy and intricate decorative effects. Today the palace is used for state visits.

BELOW: Exotic, colorful facades abound at the Palacio Nacional de la Pena. The palace was begun in 1839 under Dom Fernando II, who turned the ruins of a sixteenth-century monastery into a Romantic fantasy palace.

Stunning Sintra

North of Lisbon on the outskirts of Sintra, the palace of Queluz was built between 1747 and the 1760s for one of the sons of King João of Portugal, the heir to the throne, future King Pedro III. The fanciful, decorative quality of the exterior reflects the rococo taste of the mid-eighteenth century, with an emphasis on theatricality and whimsy. Parklike grounds with fountains and statues contribute to this effect.

This taste for opulent decoration is carried through the inside of the palace, in a seemingly endless series of halls, private chambers, and recreational rooms with gilded carvings, painted ceilings, and delicate furniture. Today, the Portuguese state receives foreign dignitaries in the palace of Queluz, and uses it for special events, celebrations, and exhibitions.

Not far from Queluz stands another Portuguese masterpiece: Pena Palace. This fantasy castle of the Romantic era stands along a rocky peak of the Serra de Sintra, overlooking the craggy scenery and in fact appearing to rise out of it. The palace was begun in 1839 under Dom Fernando II, who purchased the ruins of the sixteenth-century monastery of Nossa Senhora da Pena and used them as the basis for a Romantic fantasy palace.

This visually stunning structure is a majestic pastiche reflecting the nineteenth century's love for revival styles. The large domes and many decorative elements derive from Moorish precedents so familiar to residents of the Iberian peninsula. Gothic construction and other motifs also enliven this fairy-tale castle that appears to emerge from the rocky cliffs like a mirage. Dom Fernando sought to embellish the palace gardens with exotic tree and flower specimens from every corner of the Portuguese empire.

Both Queluz and Pena served primarily as summer residences. The mountainous region around Sintra—a town Lord Byron called "perhaps the most beautiful in the world"—is particularly stunning in the warm months, affording dramatic vistas of rolling green hills and rugged mountains for miles around.

BELOW: Eighteenth-century tiles adorn the park-like gardens of Queluz, which are replete with fountains, sculptures, and winding paths.

Iberian Dreams

Portugal's close neighbor, Spain, also boasts stunning palaces. The Royal Palace in Madrid was begun by Ferdinand VI after a devastating fire that in 1734 destroyed the old palace of the Hapsburg kings in Madrid, the Alcazar. In the new royal residence, it is not surprising that wood was used only for the palace doors, while the rest of the palace was built with nonflammable materials such as stone and stucco.

With 2800 rooms, 240 balconies, and 44 sets of stairs, the Royal Palace stands among the most grandiose palaces of Europe. Each room is filled with treasures crafted by the royal tapestry works, the Real Fábrica, as well as porcelain, furniture, gilded sculpture, and lavishly adorned ceilings. Paintings by Watteau, El Greco, Goya, Rubens, and van der Weyden also adorn the palace walls. Today the palace is used for official acts of state and special ceremonies and occasions, as the present monarchs choose to live in less formal quarters in the Zarzuela Palace in the suburbs of Madrid.

BELOW: The National Palace in Madrid, Spain counts some 2,800 rooms, making it one of the largest palaces of Europe. Today's Spanish royal family makes its home in the less formal quarters of the Zarzuela Palace, in the suburbs of Madrid

ABOVE: In one of the salons of the Royal Palace in Madrid, the Venetian artist Tiepolo painted a fantastic ceiling that gives the illusion of opening to a sky filled with mythical beings.

LEFT: At the Royal Palace in Madrid, gilded lions flank the royal thrones in a protective stance. Today this sumptuous palace is used for official state visits and functions.

There is perhaps no more imposing palace than the Escorial, a vast structure of cold gray granite standing in a treeless landscape less than an hour's drive from Madrid. The Spanish refer to this palace, with a facade nearly a quarter mile long, as the "eighth wonder of the world." Built between 1563 and 1584, the Escorial was commissioned under Philip II, the Hapsburg king of Spain. Originally it was designed as a monastery dedicated to one of Spain's national saints, San Lorenzo, and commemorated the Spanish victory over the French at Saint-Quentin at 1557.

Spanish architects Juan Bautista de Toledo and Juan de Herrera worked on the building, which is striking for its so-called *estilo desornamentado* or "undecorated style," referring to the stripped-down quality of this austere building. It is thought to represent the individual vision of Philip II, a monkish, reclusive personality who preferred to carry out his affairs of state from the privacy of his personal chambers in the Escorial rather than traveling out into his kingdom. Philip's successors in the Bourbon dynasty continued to inhabit the Escorial, but transformed a few of the cold rooms into more intimate, decorative spaces for use while staying there during their hunting exploits.

Today the Escorial holds precious books, manuscripts, and other treasures of Spanish history in its library, which also maintains the collection of Philip II intact. The impressive art collections of Philip II, including paintings by Dutch and German masters Bosch, Dürer, and Patinir, grace the walls of the Escorial's museum. The royal mausoleum holds the remains of many of the kings of Spain.

ABOVE: The Escorial appears like a mirage in the open plains outside of Madrid. This palace-monastery was constructed under King Philip II in the sixteenth century, and maintains intact his impressive collection of paintings and documents.

RIGHT: At the Palacio Nacional de la Pena in Sintra, Portugal, a fanciful sea god adorns the so-called Triton Arch.

CHAPTER THREE

LUXURY UNLEASHED: GERMANY, AUSTRIA, AND RUSSIA

From Germany eastward to Russia, with their palaces the nobility matched and sometimes topped their western neighbors in opulence, ingenuity, and luxury. At Charlottenburg Palace, for example, the design is based on the prototype of Versailles, but offers its own individual interpretation. Charlottenburg was built outside Berlin as the summer residence of Queen Sophie-Charlotte at the end of the seventeenth century. Like Versailles, the palace was based on a sprawling central building overlooking expansive gardens and a series of ponds. The living quarters of the royal family were located in the central wing of the palace, while the side wings housed annex rooms such as a concert hall, ballroom, and

RIGHT: Charlottenburg Palace near Berlin, Germany, served as the summer residence of Queen Sophie-Charlotte at the end of the seventeenth century. Its massive central building overlooks manicured gardens.

RIGHT: The palace of Sans Souci in Potsdam stands amid a 725-acre park of formal gardens. Inside the palace, Frederick the Great maintained an impressive library.

RIGHT: The rigid personality of Frederick the Great contrasted with his fanciful palace of Sans Souci in Potsdam, Germany, which reaches the heights of whimsical, rococo style.

galleries for the impressive royal porcelain collection. Though it was gutted by bombing during World War II, Charlottenburg was fully restored by 1960.

Flights of Fancy

German and Austrian palace builders achieved a pinnacle of rococo decoration by the mid-eighteenth century. Built by Frederick the Great, Sans Souci (literally "without care") represents the height of rococo style. Standing in the middle of a 725-acre park, the yellow facades and whimsical exterior sculpture lend a fanciful air to this royal palace. In addition to the customary state rooms and private chambers of the court, Sans Souci contains an impressive library commissioned by Frederick the Great.

In contrast to the fussy, capricious style of his palace, Frederick the Great himself presented a rather rigid personality. He followed a strict daily regimen that began early in the morning, when he attended to affairs of state, received foreign dignitaries, and answered correspondence. At 11:00 A.M. he inspected his regiment, followed by an elaborate midday meal that lasted up to three hours. At these gatherings, politics was

ABOVE: Taking architectural fantasy to new heights, Matthaeus Daniel Poppelman designed the Zwinger in Dresden as a pleasure pavilion for August the Strong. It was the site of countless parties, special events, and weddings.

taboo as a subject of conversation. After a walk in the palace's manicured gardens, the king worked from 4:00 to 6:00 P.M. at his desk. At 6:00 he joined court musicians on his flute for a short concert, followed by a long dinner.

Meanwhile, in Dresden, the rococo style had already taken root at the Zwinger. Best described as a "pleasure pavilion," the Zwinger takes architectural fantasy to new heights. Matthaeus Daniel Pöppelman designed this structure in 1709 for August the Strong, linking six pavilions and ponds, fountains, and lawns. August used the pavilions to host parties and special events, including the wedding of his son, Prince Friedrich August. The Zwinger is a riot of form and color, with sculpture seeming to writhe across the facades of each pavilion. It takes time for the eye to soak in the stunning variety of nymphs, scrolls, swags, and other sculpted decoration.

ABOVE: The Zwinger links six pavilions, with ponds,
fountains, lawns, sculpture, and fanciful architecture.

ABOVE: The Franconia Fountain at the Residenz Palace in Wurzburg is just one of a profusion of works of art created in the eighteenth century to decorate the sumptuous residence of the bishop-prince.

LEFT: The gardens of the Residenz Palace in Wurzburg, Germany, display some of the most dynamic sculpture of the Baroque period.

"Mad Ludwig"

King Ludwig II of Bavaria has gone down in history as one of the most eccentric personalities of any European royal dynasty. In the nineteenth century, at a time when Germany and the rest of the industrialized world emerged into the modern era, the king seemed to live in a fairy-tale world of historic grandeur. His questionable sanity and predilection toward bankrupting the royal coffers by undertaking ever more extravagant palace building projects earned him the nickname "mad Ludwig." The government relieved him of his duties in 1886, and eventually the king and his doctor were found drowned in Lake Starnberg under still-mysterious circumstances.

Whatever his mental state, Ludwig constructed three stunning palaces in the Bavarian Alps—Neuschwanstein, Linderhof, and Herrenchiemsee. The beautiful scenery of snow-capped peaks, lush evergreen forests, and green valleys set the stage for these fairy-tale palaces.

ABOVE: Linderhof—a jewel of a palace situated deep in the Bavarian woods—was the brainchild of Ludwig II. It is the smallest of his palaces, and the only one ever completed.

Neuschwanstein rises like a mirage in the midst of a pristine alpine backdrop, overlooking the Hohenschwangau valleys, with snow-covered mountains in the background. This white dream palace inspired Walt Disney to build the famous Cinderella palace in Orlando, Florida, and has served as a fictitious setting for movies and children's books. Begun in 1869, Neuschwanstein required sixteen years and hundreds of craftspeople before Ludwig found it habitable; during construction the king observed the progress of his dream palace by telescope from a neighboring hilltop. As today's top tourist site in Germany, the castle has essentially reversed the flow of money out of the national coffers that was required to build it.

Linderhof was Ludwig's favorite palace. Built between 1870 and 1879, the name of the palace derives from the name *Linder,* a farm family who had occupied the land prior to Ludwig's arrival. The palace is nestled in the verdant Graswang valley of the Bavarian mountains, a remote hideaway for this eccentric king. Linderhof is the smallest of Ludwig's palaces, and the only one to be completed. However, it is surely one of the most extravagant of his creations, appearing like a precious jewel box against a background of lush evergreen trees.

The compact, ornate palace of Linderhof was modeled on the Petit Trianon at Versailles, and indeed it includes all the lavish details of any rococo palace: endless mirrors, lavish gilded sculptures, ceiling paintings, and ornate furnishings. The surrounding gardens include magnificent fountains and manicured flower beds. Ludwig was heavily inspired by the works of Richard Wagner, and his cement Venus Grotto recreates Wagner's *Tannhäuser,* complete with wave machines, rainbows, and other spectacular effects. Inside, the king's elevator table in the dining

ABOVE: In the mysterious grotto of Linderhof Palace in Bavaria, the eccentric King Ludwig recreated Richard Wagner's *Tannhäuser,* complete with wave machines, rainbows, and other spectacular effects.

LEFT: Though constructed in the nineteenth century, Linderhof Palace in Bavaria is modeled on the riotously ornate chambers of the rococo era in France.

room submerges into a below-ground kitchen, only to reemerge filled with succulent foods ready to be served to guests.

Herrenchiemsee—King Ludwig's largest palace—is located on a small island in the Chiemsee. This Versailles-style palace comes complete with a Hall of Mirrors that, at more than three hundred feet, stretches longer than the one at Versailles itself.

It also includes the axial garden plan of Le Nôtre, complete with formal flower beds, reflecting pools, and fountains. Like Neuschwanstein, Herrenchiemsee remains incomplete. The original plans called for a full-scale replica of Versailles, but only the central portion of the palace was completed before the royal funds ran dry.

ABOVE: In the nineteenth century, King Ludwig II built Herrenchiemsee Palace on the model of King Louis XIV's Versailles, including a Hall of Mirrors even larger than its French prototype.

LEFT: A bedroom at Herrenchiemsee gives a sense of the opulence Ludwig II had in mind when he embarked on this grandiose project.

BELOW: A staircase at Herrenchiemsee includes sumptuous marble facing and sculptures inset in niches. Before the palace's completion the royal coffers ran dry, and the palace remains unfinished.

Imperial Vienna

Vienna, Austria, is home to two spectacular royal residences: the Imperial Palace and the Schönnbrun Palace. The Imperial Palace traces its origins to the Middle Ages, and served as the official residence of Austrian royalty until 1918. The medieval palace chapel survives, but the rest of the palace was expanded and reconstructed during the Renaissance and baroque periods.

Today the Imperial Palace remains the official seat of the Austrian president, serves as an international convention center, and contains various official and private quarters. The Vienna Boys' Choir performs ecclesiastical music in the palace chapel. Two museums display artistic and historical treasures from Austria and around the world.

The Schönnbrun Palace served as the summer residence of the Hapsburg kings and their courts. The Schönnbrun was originally a hunting lodge, but that structure was destroyed during the Turkish siege of 1683, and it was rebuilt between 1696 and 1730. The builders emulated the classical facade and expansive gardens of Versailles. In fact, some of the palace rooms take their names from the famous French prototype, including the Marie Antoinette room and the Gobelins room (referring to the renowned French royal tapestry factory). The name of the palace itself derives from a fountain in the formal gardens known as the "Schöner Brunnen" or "beautiful fountain."

In 1762 nine-year-old Wolfgang Amadeus Mozart and his six-year-old sister Nannerl performed for the empress at Schönnbrun. The palace remained an imperial residence into the twentieth century. In 1805 and 1809 the palace served as Napoleon's Viennese headquarters. Franz Josef died at Schönnbrun in 1918. Though the buildings were heavily damaged during the Second World War, and served as Russian and then British headquarters in the war's aftermath, the palace has been restored to its original opulence and today draws many visitors.

LEFT: Belvedere Palace–surrounded by vast gardens and dynamic Baroque sculptures–served as a royal summer retreat outside the walls of Vienna.

ABOVE: Dramatically lit against the night sky, the Imperial Palace or Hofburg of Vienna served as the residence of Austrian monarchs from the Middle Ages until the collapse of the Hapsburg Empire in 1918.

LEFT: Prince Eugene of Savoy commissioned Johann Lukas von Hildebrant to design Belevedere Palace in the early eighteenth century.

LEFT: The pastel shades of the lovely facade of Schonbrunn Palace in Vienna, Austria make a dramatic backdrop for the royal residence's formal gardens. The palace served as a summer residence for the Hapsburgs.

RIGHT: Mirabell Palace in Salzburg, Austria forms a neoclassical backdrop for fabulous gardens full of mythological statues.

Royal Russia

The Russian czars made their earliest home in Moscow. The Kremlin (literally "fortress") already existed by the Middle Ages, but by 1367 it was referred to as "White Stone" because of the appearance of its exterior walls and towers. By the end of the fifteenth century the palace was rebuilt in brick, and the palace served as the center of Russian political power and Russian Orthodox faith. Today the Kremlin remains the headquarters of the Russian president.

At the beginning of the eighteenth century Peter the Great transferred his capital from Moscow to St. Petersburg. Built alongside the Neva River between 1754 and 1764, the Winter

Palace there is one of Europe's largest palaces, with more than a thousand rooms. The palace was intended for Empress Elisabeth, Peter's daughter, but the empress died before its completion. Catherine the Great and her successors made the palace their primary residence. The structure was largely rebuilt after 1837, when fire destroyed much of the original palace.

In the vast square before the Winter Palace, a grandiose column stands as a monument erected to celebrate Russia's defeat of Napoleon in 1812 under Czar Alexander I. The palace's pale green facade, interrupted by white pilasters, creates an imposing yet beautiful backdrop for the square. A gilded onion dome with a double-headed, crowned eagle stands as a symbol of imperial power.

The Winter Palace currently houses the main galleries of the Hermitage Museum, one of the most extensive and impressive art collections in the world, rivaling the Louvre and London's National Gallery. The history of the collection parallels the history of Russian taste. Catherine the Great began the collection in 1764, when she brought 255 works of art from Berlin.

LEFT: Now part of the collections of the Hermitage Museum in St. Petersburg, Russia, this sitting room of the former Winter Palace is adorned with gilded moldings and malachite mantels and pilasters.

LEFT: A view through the triumphal arch in St. Petersburg's Palace Square affords a striking vista of the Winter Palace, which now houses the galleries of the Hermitage Museum.

FOLLOWING PAGE: The "cupid staircase" at Mirabell Palace is justly famous for its profuse decoration. Today Mirabell serves as the municipal offices of Salzburg's Burgermeister.

Later the collection grew to encompass works from ancient Egypt to the modern world, including paintings by Renaissance masters Raphael and Michelangelo, as well as works of the French Impressionists. If a visitor spent one minute before each work of art in the museum, it would take eleven years to see it all.

Reflecting a desire to retreat from the busy capital of St. Petersburg, the Russian monarchs constructed the palace of Peterhof as a summer residence beginning in 1714. Sitting along the shore of the Gulf of Finland on the Baltic Sea, this "Russian Versailles" was founded by Peter the Great. In fact, Peter had visited Versailles at the end of the seventeenth century, and ordered a palace, in his words, "better than the French king's."

The complex encompasses several palace buildings and expansive gardens with fountains, stepped terraces, manicured lawns, and flower beds. This was no small feat as the wet ground along the Baltic required extensive drainage work and

ABOVE: At Peterhof, the striking gardens necessitated extensive drainage work and the transport by barge of thousands of pounds of earth and plants.

RIGHT: This interpretation of Samson and the Lion is just one of many allegorical sculptures that adorn the extravagant gardens of Peterhof Palace.

the transport of earth and thousands of plants and trees by barge to create the gardens. Throughout the grounds, pavilions and other structures welcomed members of the royal family, their entourage, and their guests for a respite from strolling in the immense park-like grounds.

The Grand Palace—begun about 1714 and enlarged in the 1750s—serves as a focal point of Peterhof, but it is the gardens and the stunning fountains that steal

ABOVE: The dramatic palace terrace at Peterhof leads to the shores of the Gulf of Finland on the Baltic Sea.

the show. The so-called Grand Cascade, a flowing waterfall and series of fountains, empties into the Baltic Sea in a spectacular display of water, architecture, and sculpture. Many of the fountain statues have allegorical meanings. One of the sculptures of the Grand Cascade entitled *The Frightened Actaeon Running Away from His Own Dogs* was meant to represent the Swedish King Charles XII, whom Peter the Great had defeated.

Hitler's forces occupied Peterhof for twenty-seven months during World War II, and as a result the palace and gardens were nearly destroyed. Restoration began immediately in 1944, and continued for years afterward. Today the palace is a major attraction for visitors to Russia.

At the beginning of the eighteenth century, nobles began to retreat from St. Petersburg to Pushkin, building country estates in this town sixteen miles south of the capital. Pushkin became the primary summer residence of the Russian royal family,

LEFT: During World War II, Hitler's forces occupied Peterhof for 27 months and the palace was nearly destroyed. Now fully restored, the palace offers an opulent view into the past, from its formal gardens to its gilded domes.

RIGHT: Catherine the Great's palace in Pushkin, Russia, is striking for its combination of gold, blue, and white on the palace exterior.

and in the 1740s and 1750s the Catherine Palace was erected there. A grandiose plaza precedes the Catherine Palace, providing a marvelous view of this original palace crowned by golden onion domes. The magnificent facade of blue, white, and gold with stucco decoration is stunning in and of itself, but it is just a hint of the rich collection of tapestries, porcelain, and paintings that lie behind those walls.

Palatial Pleasures

The ultimate goal of palaces was to enjoy all the pleasures of life—strolling, talking, playing games, and surrounding oneself with beauty both natural and man-made. For a class with the means available for full-time recreation, the palace was a world created especially to take full advantage of these pleasures. Palace life was not always fun and games, however. Royal courts and aristocratic households have always been plagued by the political conspiracies, personal rivalries, and scandals that result from living in a close-knit, exclusive community with a lot of free time on its hands.

Through their architecture and decoration, palaces make statements of political power, military might, and social prestige. More than that, these stunning structures represent a desire on the part of their patrons for immortality. Just as writers hope that their words will reach the ears of generations to come, palace builders and patrons wish for their magical creations to last for eternity as a testament to their ingenuity and greatness. In large part it is by virtue of Versailles that Louis XIV will go down in history, and through Neuschwanstein Ludwig II of Bavaria will not soon be forgotten. These structures also form an enduring testament to the virtuosity of architects, builders, garden designers, and craftspeople throughout the centuries. Through their creations, these individuals—though many remain unnamed—achieve a certain immortality.

If the walls of each palace could speak, they would reverberate with personal stories of triumph, intrigue, success, and disaster. In a way, palace walls *do* speak. They speak in the special way in which art and architecture finds a voice that still rings loud and clear for audiences who view them centuries later. Through these fascinating monuments, we step back into history. Suddenly we find ourselves walking in the footsteps of elegant ladies in flowing gowns strolling arm and arm through manicured gardens, gliding across the ballroom floor at a masquerade ball, or sitting before an ornate desk in the great hall signing an important state document. This is the legacy that palaces bequeath to our generation. And it is an achievement of palatial proportions.

LEFT: The Catherine Palace, with its striking gilded onion domes, stands among acres of formal gardens.

RIGHT: A sumptuous hall in the Catherine Palace offers just a glimpse of some of the objects that make up a rich collection of tapestries, porcelain, sculpture and paintings.

INDEX

Page numbers in **boldface** indicate picture captions.